Hardwired
Staying Wired in a Wireless Age

Reasons

There are three reasons that I can think of to keep your computer wired these days:
- First, you may be wanting to avoid as many EMFs as possible
- Second, IYHO (In Your Humble Opinion) it's obviously more secure
- Third, you want the speed. However, if it's just speed that you want might need a faster network. https://www.speedtest.net/global-index

NASA's network is over 91GBPS (GigaBits Per Second), rather than however many MBPS (MegaBits Per Second) your current network is. Of course, NASA's network is reserved for NASA.
https://www.technopediasite.com/2019/09/7g-and-8g-network-countries.html

There may be a fourth reason. In my case it's because I'm *wired*. I mean *weird*. All four reasons apply to me.

Whatever your reasons, it is possible to keep your computer hardwired. There might also be a way to hardwire

Hardwired
Staying Wired in a Wireless Age

your cellphone through the charging port. I'll discuss that in the last chapter.

Even if hardwiring your cellphone isn't an option, there are still ways to mitigate EMFs, even with cellphones. There are also ways to make cellphones faster and more secure. These usually involve installing or removing apps, and changing settings. There are plenty of ideas about that on the web.

Tablets without connection ports fall into the same category as cellphones in this book. Tablets with ports fall into the same category as laptops.

Whatever your reasons for wanting to stay hardwired, they are valid for you. At least they're valid until / unless you discover otherwise.

Just because your laptop is hardwired, doesn't mean that you have to be chained to your desk. Nevertheless, you'll have to control when you take breaks. And if you can't control that, you may have to find a different job, one where you're not always on call.

Hardwired
Staying Wired in a Wireless Age

Terms and Definitions

Cable – The wire used to connect to each other or to a network or the internet.

Port – The place where a cable plugs into a device or the wall. I tend to think of ports as outlets. Ports are also called jacks.

EMF – ElectroMagnetic Frequency. The US National Institute of Environmental Health Sciences (NIEHS) gives their definition and findings on the effects of EMFs here: https://www.niehs.nih.gov/health/topics/agents/emf/index.cfm.

There are low level EMFs – from cellphones, etc. There are also very high level EMFs – from Power Lines and Substations. The NIEHS research says that low-level EMFs are not harmful.

In my mind, taking extra precautions to protect my health is worth it. If those precautions are unnecessary, I won't have worsened my health. Also, I know people who are severely adversely affected by low-level EMFs. Most people don't seem to notice.

Hardwired
Staying Wired in a Wireless Age

I try to listen to what my body is telling me and respond accordingly. If your body seems to be affected by EMF's, try to minimize your exposure to them. How would you know? Follow this link from the World Health Organization (WHO):
https://www.who.int/teams/environment-climate-change-and-health/radiation-and-health/non-ionizing/el-hsensitivity.

USB – Universal Serial Bus. These cables are typically used to connect devices, such as a mouse or keyboard, to a laptop.

5G – G is for generation. 1G was the first generation of Wi-Fi. That was back in 1991. Most cellphones are now 4G or 5G capable. 6G is coming, if it's not already here. Expected release date for 6G service is 2030.

The later the generation, the higher the amount of data which can be sent. And, the data can be sent at higher and higher speeds. Chances are, if you have a 3G cellphone or earlier, it doesn't work with the current 4G and 5G networks.

Network – What your cellphone carrier (company) uses to get your signal from one place to another. If you're in the US, your carrier is probably Verizon, T-Mobile, or AT&T. Possibly, it's US Cellular or some other large cellphone company that I don't know about.

Smaller cellphone companies typically use whatever larger carrier's network they can tie into. And some smaller cellphone companies are owned by the Big 3.

Hardwired
Staying Wired in a Wireless Age

Wi-Fi – Wireless Connection. Wi-Fi is the protocol (set of instructions) used to exchange data using radio waves. Most people spell Wi-Fi as *wifi*. Wi-Fi is a trademark, so I'll spell it Wi-Fi in this book.

Bluetooth – think of this as Wi-Fi for very short distances (30 feet / 10 meters or less).

Ethernet – Wired Connection to the Internet or between Computer Networks. If you're buying an Ethernet Cable, you don't need to buy the most expensive one. On the other hand, the cheapest Ethernet Cable may not give you the speed you want.

I choose Ethernet Cables which are rated as being faster. If I don't see ratings, I skip the cheapest cables and go for ones which are priced slightly higher.

RJ45 – This is typically the connector at the end of an Ethernet cable. Very, very, very fast Ethernet cables may have a GG45 connector instead. Those cables *can* take an RJ45 connector. However GG45 is backwards compatible to RJ45. And that's good, because most Ethernet ports are RJ45.

Router – Routes signals between devices or to/from the internet. Many Routers use Wi-Fi in addition to cables. Some use Wi-Fi rather than cables.

Hub – A connector which can be used to extend the length of a cable. Many Hubs use Wi-Fi in addition to cables. Some use Wi-Fi rather than cables.
A router can control the signals. Hubs don't contain that software.

Hardwired
Staying Wired in a Wireless Age

Bridges and switches are also used to connect devices to each other and to the internet / network. Netgear only sells wired switches, so maybe all switches are wired. All Netgear bridges are wireless.

I read what the internet had to say about bridges and switches. In the five seconds I took to do that, I didn't understand it. From what I *could* understand, it sounds like bridges and switches are more specialized than routers and hubs. Whatever bridges and switches are, Netgear sells them only as business, rather than personal, devices.

GPS – Global Positioning System. Tells us where we are when we're lost and sometimes when we ain't.

Hardwired
Staying Wired in a Wireless Age

Disclaimer

I'm not an electrical engineer. I can only speak from my own experience with what works for me, and as a HSP – Highly Sensitive Person – see HSPerson.com for more information.

I flunked the test on that website to see if I was an HSP. I chalk that up to my being very well grounded. So, I can sense lots of things like low-level EMFs while not being negatively affected by them to a great extent.

Those who know me well will attest that I am sensitive. And in my mind, that's a good thing. It just means that I'm more aware of things than most people.

I want the security and speed that being hardwired gives me. And I prefer to have very few drops in my internet signal, if any.

This book is about what I do to stay hardwired and my research into that subject. If it doesn't apply, it doesn't apply. If it helps, great!

I figure that there are others like me who want to stay hardwired. So, I'm partially writing this book for selfish reasons. If more people become hardwired, manufacturers

Hardwired
Staying Wired in a Wireless Age

will still produce what I need. And that will allow me to remain hardwired.

I'm not trying to persuade anyone one way or the other. I'm just letting you know that there are resources, if a hardwired lifestyle is for you.

Perhaps a hardwired lifestyle is not for you all of the time. However, you'd like to keep that option open.

I'm very familiar with most of the companies mentioned in this book. I am not getting paid by any of them.

Hardwired
Staying Wired in a Wireless Age

Table of Contents

Reasons 1

Terms and Definitions 3

Disclaimer 7

Table of Contents 9

Point of Entry 11

Connection Speeds 13

Creating a Safe Zone 15

Connecting Laptops to the Internet 20

The Keyboard 24

The Mouse 27

Does It Need to be Connected? 29

Headsets 33

Virtual Reality (VR) 37

Hardwired
Staying Wired in a Wireless Age

Keeping Cords Untangled and Organized 39
Hardwiring your Cellphone 43
SAR Ratings 45
My Recommended Cellphone Settings 47
Other Ways to Minimize Your Device's EMFs 50
About the Author 53

Hardwired
Staying Wired in a Wireless Age

Point of Entry

If you want to reduce EMFs, there are EMF Shielding Paints that you can apply. Some of these have to be electrically grounded, however you do that. These paints are super-expensive.

I don't know anything else about these paints, other than one is listed at LessEMF https://www.lessemf.com/paint.html. That website usually has reliable EMF Shielding information and resources.

This paint is for interior or exterior usage. That's great!

And, it sounds like this particular paint color is black. *Oh great! Just what I wanted, a black room!* Maybe you can paint the room a different color once this paint is dry.

For staying hardwired at the point of entry, your home will need to have an Ethernet (internet) cable. Comcast provided that cable at one of my homes. The cellphone company provided that cable at another.

Comcast and the cellphone company both then connected that cable to a router. A router routes signals between various devices.

Hardwired

Staying Wired in a Wireless Age

Comcast finally made me upgrade to a wireless router. I only agreed to do so after they assured me that I could turn off the wireless signal and use it with Ethernet cables.

To turn off the wireless signal, I had to log into the router and enter some commands. I have enough computer experience to do that. If that hadn't been the case, I would have made Comcast do that for me.

The Comcast and cellphone company routers would have wirelessly connected to several devices. However, I wanted to connect hardwired. And, the Comcast router was limited to two outgoing Ethernet cables.

I needed one for my laptop, one for my wife's, one for our printer, one for our housemate's laptop. You guessed it. That's more than two.

So, I ran one Ethernet chord from the Comcast router to my own D-Link router. Again, I had to log in and turn off the wireless on that router. That particular router had one input and three output plugs for Ethernet cables. And, that setup had worked well, until we got our housemate.

At that point, I bought a NetGear hub. Hubs are like routers, except there's no intelligence in them or not much. And, it was easy to find hubs without wireless connections.

Hubs are also less expensive than routers. Plus, they often have many more ports (places to connect cables).

I should have bought a hub with more than four ports. That way I could have just used the hub and not both the router and the hub. Live and learn, maybe.

Hardwired
Staying Wired in a Wireless Age

Connection Speeds

Various Internet providers, like Comcast, offer different connection speeds to the internet. Comcast was the only choice when I bought one of my homes, back in 2003. Since I was the first one in my neighborhood to connect to Comcast, the connection box was right outside my house.

I got the best connection speed. Those who signed up later, got a connection speed which was slightly slower.

https://www.mymove.com/broadband/guides/internet-speed/ lists connection speeds various types of connections. It lists Cable as up to 100 MBPS – MegaBits Per Second. Fiber-optic, they list as up to 2,000 MBPS. Fibre-optic is 10 times as fast as DSL. And DSL is what some cellphone companies offer.

I think that their definition of cable is different from mine. Comcast speeds were those of Fibre-optic cables. Here are their definitions https://www.allconnect.com/blog/find-internet-connection-type.

Of course, when all of the kids got out of school and logged onto their laptops, the internet got really slow, even with my setup. I noticed that Comcast later fixed this

Hardwired
Staying Wired in a Wireless Age

somehow. During COVID-19, when kids were schooling from home, I didn't notice any slowdowns at all.

I know that part of Comcast's fix was to separate heavy internet users from the rest of us, so that those users weren't clogging the network. So, perhaps all those school kids were playing videos or video games, rather than doing their homework, once they got home from school.

Hardwired
Staying Wired in a Wireless Age

Creating a Safe Zone

You may want to divide your house into various zones. Some of these might be hard-wired, no Wi-Fi allowed. In others Wi-Fi is always allowed. In some, Wi-Fi is only allowed during certain hours of the day.

And, there may be one zone where you might not want to allow any devices, not even those which are hardwired. This would be your laptop-free, TV-free, cellphone-free, device-free zone.

How you set up your home is completely up to you. You may want to totally intermix things and have no zones at all.

Some people set their bedroom aside as an EMF-free Zone. That way, they can get a good night's sleep. And their body is recharged to resist EMFs for another day. Others choose a meditation alcove where they're EMF-free for an hour or two each day. Some use an unwired outbuilding.

If you're setting aside your bedroom as a device-free zone, the first thing that is recommended, is removing everything, except your bed and yourself, from your bedroom.

Hardwired
Staying Wired in a Wireless Age

This isn't always practical. Still, you'll probably want to remove as much as possible.

The first things to remove from your bedroom are all of the electrical appliances. You might still need a lamp. So, perhaps you can't remove all of the electrical appliances. You also might need an alarm.

You might choose to keep a battery powered light and/or alarm. Yet, Battery-powered devices can also give off EMFs.

And what about that overhead lamp which you can't do anything about? If you flip the breaker for that light, you'll probably shut off electricity somewhere else where it's needed.

When you have minimized what's in your bedroom. You might notice that you have way too much space in that room. You might then decide to use a different room for your bedroom. You might even find yourself sleeping in a closet.

When you've finally settled on where you're going to sleep, and it's just you and your bed and perhaps a few other things, you'll want to check the outlets to make sure that they're wired correctly. You can also check the light-switches.

In newer houses, this may not be a concern. If you're buying a house, ask the inspector to check that. They might do without being asked. Nevertheless, it won't hurt to ask.

We bought an old house. After four tries, we finally got all of the outlets wired correctly. We only checked them to

Hardwired
Staying Wired in a Wireless Age

know which ones needed work. Then, we had electricians come out to wire them correctly and/or to ground them.

It was good that we had electricians out because the unattached ground wires were really short and hard to hook up to the outlet. We were lucky that the electricians didn't have to run additional ground wires. That would have cost us extra.

When we went to place the house on the market, we discovered yet another ungrounded outlet. It had been hidden behind something that entire time.

I suppose that we could have had the Electricians out to test the outlets. But why have them out for the outlets which were fine?

And besides, my wife had a tester which she knew how to use Outlet testers are readily available at hardware stores.

Speaking of keeping things grounded, you can purchase grounding pads. You can stick these in your bed and place your feet on them. They keep you grounded all night long.

You can purchase these at Earthing.com and elsewhere. Earthing.com also has earthing pads for your car.

These work well for my wife. I'm well enough grounded without them. And I must be wired backwards, because they cause me to be jittery if I use them for very long.

Hardwired
Staying Wired in a Wireless Age

The next recommendation for creating an EMF-Free Zone in your bedroom, is to build a Faraday Cage around your bed. These cages block out EMFs.

Building a Faraday Cage might take a Master's Degree in Construction. Plus, copper is used to make them and copper is expensive. Even so, this link will tell you one way to DIY Build a Faraday Cage.
https://mpkb.org/home/special/emf/whitezones/faradaycage

Shield Your Body and others sell bed canopies to protect you from EMFs. These are easier to install than an actual Faraday Cage. You just need to hang them over your bed, somehow.

If you're looking for something more portable, consider EMF Shielding Apparel. LessEMF and others carry that. Most EMF Shielding Apparel contains silver fibers. These fibers create a sort of Faraday Cage to protect your body. Check to see if you this clothing needs to be hand-washed or not.

If you're wanting a pre-built room, which is in and of itself a Faraday Cage, HollandShielding carries those. I have no experience with HollandShielding. I just found them on the internet. They also sell EMF Shielding Apparel.

Alternatively, I suppose you could skip the Faraday Cage and paint your bedroom black with one of those EMF Shielding Paints. You'll only be sleeping there with your eyes closed. So, why should you care what color it is?

Hardwired
Staying Wired in a Wireless Age

You can also purchase EMF Testers to verify that your EMF-Free Zone has been set up correctly. These are better known as EMF Meters.

Not only are there several brands of EMF Meters, there are also several kinds. You will probably want either a Radio Frequency Meter or a Combination Meter (which measures Radio Frequencies and EMFs from outlets (AC) and from battery powered devices (DC)). LessEMF has more information on those.

Hardwired
Staying Wired in a Wireless Age

Connecting Laptops to the Internet

Older laptops have Ethernet ports. Newer laptops often do not.

Dell lets you configure your laptop if you purchase it on their website. Unfortunately, whether your laptop has an Ethernet port or not, does not seem to be a current configuration choice.

On the other hand, Dell sells XPS, G Series, and Alienware gaming laptops. Gamers love speed. So, gaming laptops may have Ethernet ports. I just looked at Dell's first G Series laptop and at did. Asus, Lenovo, Razer, MSI, Gigabyte, and HP also sell gaming laptops.

Gaming laptops have a lot of power and a lot of speed. They *can* also cost a lot. *Can* being the operative word. They can also cost less than or as much as a non-gaming laptop. It depends on what you're comparing.

Hardwired
Staying Wired in a Wireless Age

My Samsung laptop does not have an Ethernet port. It does, however, have a port for a USB-c connection. USB-c is like USB, but smaller (more compact). It's a little, flat port.

Now you're asking yourself, *How will my Ethernet cord ever fit into that little tiny port?* Don't try shoving it in. Use an adaptor instead.

J5-Create makes this type of adaptor. Anker, Thunderbolt, and Startech also make USB-c to Ethernet adaptors / connectors. You'll want to make certain that the connector speed is in gigabits (GB) or better yet, terabits (TB).

J5-Create, Anker, Thunderbolt, and Startech have adaptors with multiple ports. J5-Create and Anker tend to only have adaptors with two USB ports and one Ethernet port. Thunderbolt and Startech have some adaptors with more than two USB ports (and one Ethernet port).

It looks like Belkin and Insignia (among others) have cable connectors. These let you use one cable to go from USB-c to Ethernet (RJ45). I haven't tried any of them. I want those extra USB-A ports.

I use a J5-Create with two USB ports. These are the large, USB-A ports. I can plug an external keyboard and a mouse into those ports. I don't need to do that though, because my laptop has two USB-A ports. And, I use those for that purpose.

My wife's newer Samsung laptop does not have those two USB-A ports. So I connected hers up by connecting the

Hardwired
Staying Wired in a Wireless Age

keyboard and the mouse through the J5-Create adapter. Everything worked.

I then tried to connect a USB-A hub (cord connector) to the J5-Create and then connect the keyboard and mouse through that. I wanted an extra port to connect her USB Salt Crystal Lamp to her computer. I'll explain more about that later.

No matter what I tried, it wouldn't work. Finally, I noticed the USB-c (smaller) power connection on the J5-Create. And it's a good thing I did, because nobody at J5-Create or Anchor or BestBuy could tell me why nothing worked the way I had things set up.

When I connected a plugged-in cellphone power cable to the J5-Create, everything worked. Even though neither the keyboard, nor the mouse, nor even some of the hubs I tried required power, I still had to power the J5-Create or nothing worked, not even the internet connection through the Ethernet cable in the J5-Create.

Now that there was power, everything worked. However, due to the distance of the outlet from the laptop, I had to buy a cellphone charger with a longer cable.

It's too bad that I didn't come across a Thunderbolt or Startech adaptors at that time. Then, I could have had at least 4 USB ports along with my Ethernet port. And, I would have been in seventh heaven, provided everything worked and I didn't encounter other complications.

Hardwired

Staying Wired in a Wireless Age

So, as long as you have a USB-c port on your laptop or better yet an Ethernet port, you're all set. You can connect hardwired.

Tablets, laptop's smaller cousins, didn't use to have ports for anything. Now manufacturers are adding USB-c ports to some models. This means, with a newer tablet which has USB-c ports, you will be able to once again connect to the Internet and stay wired.

What's the difference between a tablet and a laptop? See https://www.lifewire.com/tablets-vs-laptops-832333.

Since I use my laptop for business, I'll be sticking with a laptop, rather than a tablet. I need the extra memory, space, etc.

Nevertheless, I might consider a 2-in-1 laptop that I can use in either laptop or tablet mode. Yet, I wouldn't be detaching the screen unless somehow I could detach it and keep it wired.

Besides, if I did detach the screen, I'd probably lose track of where I left the rest of the laptop. And then I'd be in big trouble. I wonder if there's a button that you can push to find out where the rest of your laptop is.

Hardwired
Staying Wired in a Wireless Age

The Keyboard

You may be fine using the keyboard which comes with your laptop. You might even use the screen keyboard which is available on some touch screens.

Yes, I can use the keyboard which comes with my laptop. I haven't tried using a screen keyboard, except on my cellphone. There are a few reasons that I don't use these options.

First, I like a larger keyboard. I like the 104-key keyboard. I especially like its numeric 10-key pad.

I do wish that the keyboard came in three rearrangeable plug-and-play sections:
- One for the number keys
- One for the arrow key section, and
- One for the rest of the keyboard.

I'd like to place the arrows on the left and the numbers on the right. That way, I wouldn't have to move my hand so far to use the numeric 10-key pad.

The second reason that I don't use a laptop keyboard, is that I like to raise my screen without raising the keyboard, it's better for me, ergonomically speaking. There are 2-in-1

Hardwired
Staying Wired in a Wireless Age

laptops now which allow you to detach the keyboard from the screen. Yet, as far as I know, in that case, you have to use the touchscreen's keyboard.

I just use cardboard boxes to raise my laptop so that I don't have to look down at my screen quite so much. And, I use an external keyboard so that I can keep it at a separate level from the laptop.

I learned to type on a manual typewriter. Yes, I'm that old. This particular typewriter had a 14-inch carriage return and typing area. It was made for typing newspapers. Not that I ever did that.

That carriage return was very heavy. And it probably needed to be oiled. You had to shove it across from right to left when you wanted to go to the next line.

The keys on this typewriter were very stiff. Again, they probably needed to be oiled. Your fingers had to be very strong to use it.

I still type full-strength, so to speak. I have broken more than one keyboard, over extended periods of time. Usually the space bar is the first to go. That's another reason I use an external keyboard.

I haven't ruined any keyboards on my laptop yet. However, I don't use them very often.

I swype on my cellphone, which takes much less pressure than typing did on that old manual keyboard. And so far, my cellphone is fine.

Hardwired
Staying Wired in a Wireless Age

Swyping means that you trace the word you want to type by dragging your finger on the keyboard from the first letter of that word to the next, and so forth, on to the last letter. There was originally a Swype keyboard *app* available on Android phones. That company went out of business. Notwithstanding that, swyping was available on most other keyboards by that time.

I do fairly well with swyping. I might do better if my fingers were skinnier. Sometimes I can't quite get the cursor to go where I want it to go.

Apple calls swyping QuickPath. QuickPath is available on iPhones and iPads.

Hardwired
Staying Wired in a Wireless Age

The Mouse

I can use the mousepad (touchpad) on my laptop, rather than a mouse, but not very well. If I get within an inch or two of the mousepad with my fingers, it thinks that they are right on top of it. It even thinks this, when the sensitivity is set as low as possible. I am also more accurate with a mouse than I am with the mousepad.

With a touchscreen, I don't need to use either a mouse or a touchpad. However, I still prefer to use a mouse.

There are those little mouseballs in the middle of some keyboards. I can't get any accuracy with those. And they're always in my way. These are actually called *pointing sticks*.

Perhaps I could do better with a track ball or joystick. I've never tried either of those.

Perhaps if I took the time, I could get used to using the mousepad in spite of that sensitivity issue. It took me over a year to get used to using a mouse back in 1991. They've improved over the years, as has my ability to maneuver them.

Sometimes I have to work in an office where my laptop is connected to the network via Wi-Fi. Even then, I use a

Hardwired

Staying Wired in a Wireless Age

wired mouse due to the complications mentioned above. I only use an external keyboard in those instances, when I can fit it into my suitcase.

I developed an idea to combine the keyboard and the mouse into two-mice, each with five buttons. Read <u>In Search of a Right-Brained Computer</u>, if you want to have a laugh and find out more about that.

Many mice and keyboards these days are wireless. And it used to be that you had to order these devices wired, since stores only carried them online and not in their brick and mortar stores.

Logically, it might make more sense to carry wireless devices in a virtual store and vice-versa. But I don't make those rules.

Now, you can sometimes find wired mice and keyboards (more likely mice) in physical stores. That's because some gamers prefer them. Turns out that wired devices are slightly faster than wireless ones.

A gaming mouse may be more than you need. And it may well cost more than you want to spend. But at least they're available. On the other hand, if you want a non-gaming wired mouse, you're probably going to have to order it online.

Hardwired
Staying Wired in a Wireless Age

Does It Need to be Connected?

There are some USB devices that perhaps do not need to be connected to your computer or the Internet. Take that USB salt crystal lamp which I mentioned earlier, for instance. Yes, it's USB so that it runs on low power. And yes, it's smaller and less expensive than normal size, non-USB salt crystal lamps.

Even taking all of that into consideration, you don't need to run the USB salt crystal lamp off of your computer. You can just plug it into the base of a cellphone charger instead. Perhaps it came with one.

If you're buying a new charger for this purpose, make certain that you buy one which allows the cord to be detached from the base. Make sure that you don't buy one which is all one piece. If you do, you won't have a place to plug in the salt crystal lamp.

Our J5-Creates only have two USB ports. I only need one for my keyboard and one for my mouse. I'm set. If I need to charge my cellphone, I always plug it in to its

Hardwired
Staying Wired in a Wireless Age

charger for fast charging, rather than trying to charge it off of my laptop.

What else is there? Oh yes, that salt crystal lamp or perhaps external speakers or webcams.

There are some one-to-two cable cables. These are called splitter cables. But why limit yourself to two, when you can buy a USB hub (or USB hub splitter, same thing) and connect several devices.

Just make sure that you get what you need. USB comes in both USB and USB-c (compact). Even though the *U* is for *Universal*, one size does not fit all. But you already knew that *U* didn't really mean *Universal* the first time you tried to plug in your USB cord and discovered that you had to flip it over.

Actually, the original plan for USB cords and ports was to build them so that you didn't have to flip the cord over. However, it would have cost more to build them that way. That, in turn, would have made the price too high. And we've been stuck with uni-directional universal serial buses (USB) forever since.

There are also USB-b connectors and ports. Those are for connecting printers. There are mini versions of USB-a and USB-b. There are also different versions for USB version 3 versus for earlier versions.
https://en.wikipedia.org/wiki/USB_hardware

So, what did they mean when they called their cables and ports *Universal*? I'm not sure, but I think that they might have meant *more Universal*. Also USB-a was much more Universal. And in the beginning, that's all there was. USB-b came along later, and then USB-c.

Hardwired
Staying Wired in a Wireless Age

Many years ago, my uncle thought about setting up a shop to make and sell cables. Back then, cables were very expensive. And they were not Universal at all.

Just when he was about to start moving forward with that idea, cables became more standardized and less expensive.

All of that happened a long time before USB cables came into existence. Perhaps, if my uncle had stuck with his idea, he would have invented USB cables, rather than Ajay Bhatt and Intel.

Other USB devices that you might be interested in which don't need to be connected, might include:
- Fan
- Heater
- Lamp, something other than the already mentioned salt crystal lamp. Perhaps a flexlight.
- Piano keyboards
- Beverage Cooler
- Coffee Warmer
- Rice Cooker
- Air purifiers
- Computer vacuums

Some of these gadgets may be hard to find. Many of the quirkier ones look like they were a one-time production,

There are many quirkier products, including the USB pet rock. What a rock, either wild or domestic, would do with a USB connection is beyond me.

Hardwired

Staying Wired in a Wireless Age

Turns out that USB Pet Rocks are still for sale. It also turns out that they don't do anything thing with their USB connection. It just exists for amusement.

Nevertheless, you'll want to make certain you have the USB connection plugged in to a power source. That way, your friends won't see through your spoof.

https://www.amazon.ca/ThinkGeek-USB-Pet-Rock/dp/B00A9TH6B8

Hardwired
Staying Wired in a Wireless Age

Headsets

So, you're sitting at your computer, which is now all hard-wired. And your favorite song is blasting at 1,000 decibels. You're in the zone!

Then your roommate, or possibly somebody a mile away, yells, *Turn that down! I can't hear myself think! Are you trying to go deaf?*

In order to keep the peace, you start to plug in your earphones or headset. But then you worry that those EMFs are heading right up that wire from your computer, straight into your brain.

What to do? What to do? What to do?

I know of two options. The first option is a set of Airtubes. Airtubes in this case are earphones. There are many other products that are called Airtubes. I'm not talking about them.

The second option is the HARD protection headset adapter. This is a connector between your laptop and your headset.

Hardwired
Staying Wired in a Wireless Age

Airtubes are made by multiple companies. LessEMF sells one, as does Dr Mercola. You may need an adapter to hook them to your cellphone.

On the other hand, you may not be able to hook them to your cellphone at all, if your cellphone doesn't have a place to plug in earphones.

That seems to be the current trend. However several cellphones still have headphone jacks (ports). https://www.androidauthority.com/phones-with-headphone-jack-825984/

Also, there are USB-c headphones that you can plug into the charging port of your cellphone. Your Airtubes may have come with a USB-c adaptor. If not, you can buy one online.

I couldn't get Airtubes to work for me (volume-wise) until I switched the tips. (Tips are those little things which go in your ears and allow you to hear what's coming through the Airtubes). My Airtubes came with various sizes of tips. So, I didn't have to buy new ones.

The tips which were attached to the Airtubes when they were shipped to me, wouldn't fit in my ears far enough for me to hear anything. Of course, on the other hand, I didn't want my Airtube tips to be small enough that they could get lost in my ear canals. I did manage to find the correct size among the provided tips.

Note: Some Airtubes are called headsets. They are probably earbuds. The only over-the-ear Airtubes that I can find are by iBrain.

Hardwired

Staying Wired in a Wireless Age

The HARD protection headset adapter is made by Shield Your Body. It stops EMFs from traveling through it into your headsets. Shield Your Body also makes Airtubes and a laptop EMF shield which you place under your laptop.

I think that the HARD protection headset adapter works with both headsets and earbuds. It appears that way. You just plug the adapter into your laptop. Then you plug the headset into the adapter.

If you want to really be hardwired, you can plug your Airtubes into the HARD adaptor. However, going that far might be a little extreme, even for me.

One note about over-the-ear headsets. I had to buy a new pair of glasses when I got my headsets. I could put my headsets on over the earpieces of my glasses just fine.

However, if I took off my glasses, I couldn't put them back on without removing the headsets first. And that didn't work well during meetings.

Turns out that the ends of the earpieces of my glasses were too fat. I had to buy a new pair of glasses with much skinnier earpiece ends. I found some which had earpiece ends which were very small.

Buying those new glasses didn't cost me an arm and a leg, because I buy my glasses online https://www.princesstigerlily.com/search/glasses.html. Even so, I had to search several websites until I found a pair which didn't look like the earpieces would poke me in the head every time I put them on.

Hardwired
Staying Wired in a Wireless Age

If you don't wear glasses, you may be wondering why I took them off during the meeting in the first place. Usually it was to clean them. Occasionally, it was so that I could read some really fine print. Sometimes, it might have been so that I could focus on something which was further away from me than the computer screen.

Hardwired
Staying Wired in a Wireless Age

Virtual Reality (VR)

Speaking of glasses, brings up a new question. Are there still any wired virtual reality (VR) devices? In 2021, wireless VR was in its infancy, according to this article. https://www.expertreviews.co.uk/technology/1405721/best-vr-headset

The specs for the HTC Vive Cosmos VR listed in that article, say that the headset is hardwired. It doesn't say if the controllers are also hardwired.

Most VR headsets I looked at online, look like they are wireless. However, it may be that the wires are just not being shown in the pictures.

If you really want to have a wired virtual experience, you're going to have to do a lot more investigation. Perhaps you will need to chat with a few manufacturers.

I experienced VR a few years ago at the Kennedy Space Center Visitor Complex in Florida (near Cape Canaveral). Buzz Aldrin took our group on a tour of Mars.

While the tour was interesting, it wasn't very virtual. I still weighed as much as I did back on Earth.

Hardwired
Staying Wired in a Wireless Age

I don't think that I'll be trying VR again any time soon. My life has enough virtual reality in it as it is, without any help from devices.

Hardwired
Staying Wired in a Wireless Age

Keeping Cords Untangled and Organized

If you are traveling with your wired laptop and all of its cords and all of your laptops peripherals and all of their cords, you might want to keep them all from getting tangled. You might not want them to get tangled together or to get tangled with themselves.

I'm fine if they get tangled. I'm patient enough to untangle them. On the other hand, I'm not patient enough to try and coil them up and fasten them with twist-ties or some such to keep them from getting tangled.

Some of the following ideas may help you keep your cords untangled, if you want to do that. Some may also help you keep your cords organized.

https://www.onecrazyhouse.com/diy-cord-organizers/ tells simple and sometimes free ways to keep your cords organized. Do they really work?

Hardwired
Staying Wired in a Wireless Age

The first one – keep your cords in toilet paper roll tubes, once they no longer host toilet paper. It seems to me like it would be difficult to get the cords in and out. And, I'd probably get papercuts from the cardboard tubes in the process. So, I'm not even going to try that idea.

The second idea – place bread ties on the plugin part of power cords and then label those ties. That idea might work, if you're adept at working bread ties. I am not.
Also, I can't write neatly. So, labeling the ties? I'd have to get somebody else to label them for me.

Idea #8 – Binder Clips. Now that looks like it might work.

#13 – Ziploc bags – another good idea until the bag or loc wears out. If the bags are new, they'll probably last the length of your trip.
Then again, I don't know where you're going or how long you'll be gone for. I don't know what you'll be doing on your trip or if gorillas will be handling your baggage. So then again, they might not last that long.

#14 Legos characters. Dare I admit that it's been so long since I played with Legos that characters didn't exist, just simple bricks and maybe chimney bricks.
If I did go this route of using Legos characters, I'd have to choose Emmet or maybe a Robot. For smaller-width cables, the mini figures set might work best.
It looks like most of the characters are not sold separately. So, I would have to buy an entire set. And then I'd have to play with them. And that would never do, not at my age.

Hardwired
Staying Wired in a Wireless Age

https://www.travelfashiongirl.com/travel-cord-organizer/ looks to me to have better ideas. I like the Velcro ties the best.

Etsy.com looks like it has things which are better suited to organizing your cords. Plus, many of those are much cuter. Most of those, however are too small for the laptop cord itself.

Just search for *cord organizer travel*. *Cord holder* is another good search phrase. You'll find some ideas.

---

https://www.peakdesign.com/products/tech-pouch. This Tech Pouch by Peak Design has lots of pockets to help you keep things organized. However, I'm known for Packing Petite. And, this pouch would take more room than what I would put into it.

If it's a pouch that you're looking for to fit all of your cords into, https://upgradedpoints.com/travel/best-travel-cable-cord-organizers/ looks like it has a good list.

Like I said, I'm not going to bother to try and keep my cords tangle-free. Untangling the cords keeps me from getting bored. It also keeps my fingers flexible, so that I can write more books.

As for organized, they may look messy. Nevertheless, just because they look messy doesn't mean that I don't

Hardwired
Staying Wired in a Wireless Age

know where each and every cord is. That's organized enough for me.

It may not look organized to others. However, there are many different organizational methods. I try to use the one which works for me. That's much less stressful than using one which doesn't.

Hardwired
Staying Wired in a Wireless Age

Hardwiring your Cellphone

Here's a video https://www.youtube.com/watch?v=7rQ8h0UJvx0 which says that it's possible to hardwire your cellphone. The video warns that doing this will eat up the life of your cellphone's battery.

Perhaps, you could use a J5-Create that's plugged in, rather than the adaptor that the creator of video used. Then, perhaps, hardwiring your cellphone would work.

This video only shows a speed test which downloads and uploads data from the internet. It doesn't say if hardwiring works for calling or texting.

Here's a great article on hardwiring your cellphone https://www.pcmag.com/how-to/connect-phone-tablet-to-internet-ethernet-cable. It also doesn't say if hardwiring works for calling or texting.

This article further explains that for Android phones, you'll need a USB-c to Ethernet adaptor (either a short cable or a J5-Create or similar), unless your cellphone is

Hardwired
Staying Wired in a Wireless Age

really old. In that case you'll need a USB-a to Ethernet adaptor. If you have an iPhone, you'll need a Lightning to Ethernet adaptor.

There are several free texting apps that will work on your laptop. Since those apps use a different phone number from your cellphone, you may not be able to sync your messages. And that might get confusing.

However, if you're only using your cellphone to text, and you have a laptop, you might want to consider one of these apps. Then you can get rid of your cellphone and save some money.

If the only other reason you're using your cellphone, is for the camera and perhaps the flashlight, you can cancel your service and still use your cellphone for those things, in theory. Of course you won't be able to send the pictures to anyone, unless you transfer them to your laptop first.

Hardwired
Staying Wired in a Wireless Age

SAR Ratings

One thing that you can do to minimize the EMF range of a device, is to check the SAR rating (Specific Absorption Rate) of that device. The SAR rating will tell you if your devices (laptops, phones, etc.) are rated high or low in EMFs.

The FCC (US Federal Communications Commission) sets the maximum SAR rating for cellphones at 1.6. The maximum in Canada and South Korea is also 1.6. Most other countries set the maximum at 2. That, in my mind, is very low. So that helps.

Usually manufacturer websites will rate their phones. Various other websites rate many different brands of phones. Laptop ratings are harder to find.

Many Samsung cellphones usually end up on the low end of lists of cellphone EMF ratings. They're usually less than 0.3 SAR.

Some Samsung cellphones also end up on the higher end of those lists. Still, those ratings are still less than 1 SAR. You can check the SAR value of your Samsung cellphone at https://www.samsung.com/sar/sarMain.do.

Hardwired
Staying Wired in a Wireless Age

For all cellphones, Microsoft provides a tool which will tell you the SAR Rating. https://support.microsoft.com/en-us/hardware-sar-information. The following website – https://pongcase.com/blog/understand-find-specific-absorption-rate-sar-mobile-device/ – provides links to other similar websites.

Hardwired
Staying Wired in a Wireless Age

My Recommended Cellphone Settings

I turn on Airplane mode on my cellphone whenever possible. This may be called Flight Mode, Aeroplane Mode, Offline Mode, or Standalone Mode on other cellphones.

Airplane mode automatically turns off my Wi-Fi and Bluetooth. You may need to manually turns yours off.

If I'm on an airplane and I want to connect my cellphone to their internet, I turn Wi-Fi back on while my phone is in Airplane mode. I also plug in my cellphone, so that the currently playing movie doesn't drain my battery. That is I plug it in, provided I can reach that plug.

I carry the few things I might need while I'm on the plane in a small organizing bag that easily fits in both my carry-on and in the back seat pouch on the airplane. Mine is bright pink, so that I won't forget it. These few things include airtubes and phone charger. The cellphone is still in my hand from when I used it to board.

Hardwired

Staying Wired in a Wireless Age

I use a Yoobi pencil case (carrier). I must say though, that I prefer their current Marvel Avenger's version. https://yoobi.com/collections/avengers/products/school-bus-pencil-case.

The Captain Marvel pencil case is also pretty neat (IMHO). However, it's not sold on the Yoobi website. https://www.target.com/p/zipper-pencil-case-barrel-captain-marvel-yoobi-8482/-/A-81582513#lnk=sametab

Normally, when I'm on an airplane, I usually sleep. When I'm awake, I might talk to the passengers next to me, provided they're willing to talk. I might also look out the window, provided there's anything to see and somebody else doesn't object.

Some apps may require Wi-Fi. Cellphone assistants – Siri, Alexa, Google Assistant, and Bixby– are among those https://www.androidauthority.com/best-personal-assistant-apps-android-667299/.

Siri is finally moving away from requiring an internet connection https://www.theverge.com/2021/6/7/22522993/apple-siri-on-device-speech-recognition-no-internet-wwdc. Google Assistant beat that move by a couple of years. And Bixby was even a couple of years ahead of Google.

One article suggested that these apps might turn on Wi-Fi for you. I don't use them, so I can't check that out. If you use any app that you know will turn on Wi-Fi automatically, I would suggest disabling that permission.

Hardwired
Staying Wired in a Wireless Age

You might want to turn off that app instead. Perhaps, you'll want to uninstall it if possible.

I leave my Bluetooth off. I don't have other devices that I want to connect to my cellphone. Nor, do I want to connect other devices to my laptop. No matter how many times Windows asks.

I also turn off location. I don't know if that limits EMFs or not. But, it does take more energy. And, there is at least one GPS antenna in your cellphone. So, turning off location, might turn off that antenna. And then, at least that antenna won't be generating EMFs.

I also leave location off, because I'm under the probably false assumption, that it will be harder to track me that way. Not that I'm trying to deceive law information. Just everybody else who wants to track my every move.

I only charge my cellphone by plugging it in. I never charge it wirelessly.

I don't carry my cellphone in my pocket unless it's in airplane mode and Wi-Fi and Bluetooth are off. And I try not to hold my cellphone next to my ear when I'm using it as a phone. I turn on the speaker instead.

Hardwired
Staying Wired in a Wireless Age

Other Ways to Minimize Your Device's EMFs

There are EMF shielding devices for phones and laptops. There are also various crystals and other things that you can wear to minimize the effects of EMFs. As far as I can tell, efficacy of these things varies with the user. So, I'm not going to recommend any.

Some of these devices and crystals and ... attach to your cellphone. Others just sit somewhere near your cellphone. So, if you move your cellphone, you might have to move the device. It depends on how far you move your cellphone.

I have tried a few of these and have gotten great results. Other people whom I know have gotten questionable or negative results with the same shields. Sometimes they get no results.

There may be times when you need to have the Wi-Fi turned on. For instance, the only way to use your cellphone for communication in some locations is to have its Wi-Fi

Hardwired
Staying Wired in a Wireless Age

turned on. Some cellphones may also need auxiliary Wi-Fi turned on from some other source.

To minimize the effects of the EMFs in this situation, hold the cellphone away from your body. Turn on the speaker. And set it down.

Sometimes you're in a crowd. And turning on the speaker would be impolite.

In those situations, I get as far away from the crowd as possible. I turn the volume down and the speaker on. Then I hold the cellphone down and away from my mouth, somewhere between eight inches and a foot.

Some people recommend holding cellphones away from certain areas of your body. These include your head, reproductive areas, and belly.

Some of these people also recommend that you point the cellphone's antenna away from these areas of your body. The problem with this part of the recommendation is that today's cellphones usually have at least five antennas. If you place one antenna next to another, they can cancel each other out. So, the antennas are placed throughout the cellphone.

If all of the antennas point in the same general direction and you know which direction that is, you can point your cellphone's antennas away from you. I have no idea how to find that out.

Some of these same principles for minimizing EMF ranges also apply to laptops. I keep my laptop in airplane

Hardwired

Staying Wired in a Wireless Age

mode. I make an exception to this when I need to. For instance, I may be traveling and I need to connect to the internet somewhere where there's only a wireless connection.

When I find myself in these situations, I try to limit the amount of time that I'm connected to the internet wirelessly. I can do a lot on my computer without being connected to the internet.

For instance, I can turn on the Wi-Fi and sync my emails. Then I can place my laptop back in airplane mode (which means the Wi-Fi is off) while I go through my 200 or so emails. I can compose replies completely offline. Then, I can turn the Wi-Fi back on and send those three or four replies and perhaps a new email or two.

Turning the Wi-Fi on and off can take time. And it means that you have to concentrate on what you're doing, at least a little bit. However, if you're in an airport which charges you for the amount of time that you're connected to their Wi-Fi, this can save you a little bit of money.

Yes, you can go to the bar and usually use their Wi-Fi network for free. But then you're paying for the booze and not really saving any money. Yet, if you were going to drink anyway, that may not be a consideration.

Hardwired
Staying Wired in a Wireless Age

About the Author

I have been a Highly Sensitive Person (HSP) all my life. However, being sensitive in some areas took focus and self-training. Being sensitive in these areas didn't just come naturally. Neither was it forced into me.

Sometimes, developing sensitivities in certain areas just took repetition. One example of this is that I became able to tell when cigarette ashes had been dumped in the bussing tray without looking. Being able to tell whether a drink was a coke or a root beer, just by touching the glass, probably also came about by repetition.

At the beginning of this book, I listed my reasons for wanting my laptop to be hardwired. However, I listed them in reverse order of importance to me. I just like being hardwired. Call it habit. Call it being weird, if you want.

I really, really, like the speed. I like the sense of security that it gives me. And finally, I don't care to be engulfed by EMFs all the time.

Your reasons for being hardwired will have their own order of importance. And they may include other reasons that I forgot to mention.

Hardwired
Staying Wired in a Wireless Age

As for EMF Sensitivity. I notice when I'm not responding well to a EMFs. Usually, this is due an older home-grown Wi-Fi setup. It's energy field is jittery for some reason. I don't encounter these too often.

I can also tell when certain EMF Shields are taming down the field for me. I can sometimes tell when they'll tame down the field for someone else. So, reducing the EMF range is not that important to me, for myself.

I write books. Surprise! Surprise!

Some of them, like this one are about computers. One is a romance between a robot and a human – fast forward several years in time, maybe a century or two.

In addition to Romances and Computer books, I write Earthwise and Spiritual books. I also write books in many genres, including Fantasy, Children's, Sci-Fi, Fiction, etc. I write about several things, including superheroes, wee people (fairies, etc.), princesses, families, time travel, shape shifters, travel, even in outer space, telepathy, colors, and food.

I love doing research on topics which interest me, like this one. One of my favorite topics is Electric Cars. I've been following them for over 50 years. (Oops, aging myself again.) And I've written two books about them.

What's in the works for my books? There are some Romances. Another one on Electric Vehicles is in the initial stage.

Hardwired
Staying Wired in a Wireless Age

I'm working on another computer book. However, I need to finish coding what it's about first. So, that may take some time.

I'm also writing Fantasy, Children's, SciFi, etc. There's probably another Young Adult story in the works somewhere.

Who knows which book will get to the finish line and be published first? This book was in my *questionable* stack as of last month. Yet, somehow it has jumped to the front of the line.

Hardwired: Staying Wired in a Wireless Age was competing with a Romance to see which of them gets published first. Hardwired is much shorter. And that's probably why it won.

www.ingramcontent.com/pod-product-compliance
Lightning Source LLC
Chambersburg PA
CBHW050312220526
45465CB00005B/1958